ISBN: 9798411756074

Thank you for traveling with us!

We designed this journal to enhance your seven-week *Journey to Joy* Bible study book. We have been praying for you. Our prayer is that this journey will be transformational, bringing you to a closer relationship with your Lord and Savior.

We pray that your journaling, meditation, studying, and reading will help you move toward the joy God intended for you. Your investment of time will lead you to the abundant life Jesus spoke of when He said, "I came that they may have life and have it abundantly" (John 10:10 ESV).

Here is how the journal works. First, read the day's entry from the book. You will find two summary quotes from the book and a Bible verse. You can use the journal to answer the questions from the book on the "Reflections from the Road" page. Take notes, record your thoughts, describe your emotions, and chart your progress.

If you would like to join a *Journey to Joy* Bible Study, please email Leigh@youngandassociates.com. You can also call 828.691.0586. Study videos are located at https://www.youtube.com/c/LeighYoung.

Thank you for journeying and journaling along with us.

Joyfully yours,
Kathryn and Leigh

Week 1

Notes

Notes

'Saul! Saul! Why do you persecute me?'
'Who are you, Lord?' I asked.
'I am Jesus of Nazareth, whom you are persecuting,' he replied.

'What shall I do, Lord?' I asked.
'Get up,' the Lord said, 'and go into Damascus.
There you will be told all that you have been assigned to do.'

Acts 22:6-10

Spend some time pondering why you are taking this journey of joy and what you hope to get out of it. Studies show you are more likely to stick with a new endeavor if you know why you are doing it.
Write down your "why" for this journey.

_____

_____

_____

_____

_____

_____

_____

_____

_____

_____

_____

_____

_____

_____

"Who are you, Lord?" "What shall I do, Lord?"

Reflections from the Road

_____

_____

_____

_____

_____

_____

_____

_____

_____

_____

_____

_____

_____

_____

_____

_____

_____

_____

Lingering at the trailhead gives us the time to assess a course that will bring lasting joy.

Search me, God, and know my heart;
test me and know my anxious thoughts.
See if there is any offensive way in me,
and lead me in the way everlasting.

Psalm 139:23-24

Tuesday

Where are you on your journey to joy? Use the prompts
from the book if they are helpful in defining your current
location on the path

_____

_____

_____

_____

_____

_____

_____

_____

_____

_____

_____

_____

_____

_____

_____

_____

"We need to begin with the end in mind.

Reflections from the Road

_____
_____
_____
_____
_____
_____
_____
_____
_____
_____
_____
_____
_____
_____
_____
_____
_____
_____

As Christians, we are blessed to have a God who goes before us, understands the destination, and leads us in the right direction.

Your word is a lamp for my feet,
a light on my path.

Psalm 119:105

Wednesday

Do you have trouble believing that God loves you, and that He wants you to be happy? If you have mental blocks against these statements, describe them. If you don't, write about your background that has led you to be secure in believing these truths.

_____

_____

_____

_____

_____

_____

_____

_____

_____

_____

_____

_____

_____

_____

_____

_____

_____

_____

God's plan is for us to be joyful.

Reflections from the Road

_____

_____

_____

_____

_____

_____

_____

_____

_____

_____

_____

_____

_____

_____

_____

_____

_____

_____

_____

The God who created everything and can have anything,
desires you.

In the beginning was the Word,
and the Word was with God,
and the Word was God.
He was with God in the beginning.

John 1:1-2

Write out today's verse below:

_____

_____

_____

_____

_____

_____

_____

_____

_____

_____

_____

_____

_____

_____

_____

_____

_____

The Word of God and the God of the Word show us the path to an abundant and joyful life.

Reflections from the Road

God values us so much that He sent his Son to save us
and show us the way.

Brothers and sisters,
I do not consider myself yet to have taken
hold of it.
But one thing I do:
Forgetting what is behind and
straining toward what is ahead,
I press on toward the goal to win the prize
for which God has called me in Christ Jesus.

Philippians 3:13-14

Friday

List five things for which you are grateful this week and three things you learned from this week of study.

_____

_____

_____

_____

_____

_____

_____

_____

_____

_____

_____

_____

_____

_____

_____

Happiness is not the result of wealth.

Reflections from the Road

_____

_____

_____

_____

_____

_____

_____

_____

_____

_____

_____

_____

_____

_____

_____

_____

_____

_____

We need a new vision of joy that is clear, pure, and correct.

Week 2

Notes

Notes

_____

_____

_____

_____

_____

_____

_____

_____

_____

_____

_____

_____

_____

_____

_____

_____

_____

_____

*For I have learned to be content
whatever the circumstances.*

Philippians 4:11

Monday

In what have you been seeking your satisfaction?
How can you shift that to Jesus?

_____

_____

_____

_____

_____

_____

_____

_____

_____

_____

_____

_____

_____

_____

_____

_____

_____

_____

Joy blossoms from time with Jesus..

Reflections from the Road

True joy comes from rejoicing in the Lord, not in circumstances.

Truly I tell you,
it is hard for someone who is rich
to enter the kingdom of heaven.
Again I tell you,
it is easier for a camel to go
through
the eye of a needle
than for someone who is rich
to enter the kingdom of God.

Matthew 19:23-24

Tuesday

What have you been taking credit for that you need to give the credit back to God? How can you do so today?

_____

_____

_____

_____

_____

_____

_____

_____

_____

_____

_____

_____

_____

_____

_____

_____

_____

Rejoice and delight in the Lord in the best and the worst of times.

Reflections from the Road

_____
_____
_____
_____
_____
_____
_____
_____
_____
_____
_____
_____
_____
_____
_____
_____
_____
_____
_____

Joy can slip away when we allow ease and comfort to lull us into self-absorbed, empty pursuits which turn our focus from the Lord.

Now I want you to know,
brothers and sisters,
that what has happened to me
has actually served to advance the gospel.

Philippians 1:12

Wednesday

Do you need to introduce some struggle into your life? For example, waking up early or beginning an exercise routine can be a struggle but can produce positive health benefits. What is a habit that may seem unpleasant but could produce strength in your life? Make a plan to begin it.

_____

_____

_____

_____

_____

_____

_____

_____

_____

_____

_____

_____

_____

_____

_____

_____

Rejoice and delight in the Lord in the best and the worst of times.

Reflections from the Road

Struggles can bring joy as they strengthen.

[S]uffering produces perseverance;
perseverance, character;
and character, hope.
And hope does not put us to shame,
because God's love has been
poured out into our hearts through the Holy
Spirit,
who has been given to us.

Romans 5:3-5

Thursday

Write out today's verse below:

_____

_____

_____

_____

_____

_____

_____

_____

_____

_____

_____

_____

_____

_____

_____

_____

_____

Detours can provide the contrast we need to garner appreciation for the situations we are experiencing.

Reflections from the Road

_____

_____

_____

_____

_____

_____

_____

_____

_____

_____

_____

_____

_____

_____

_____

_____

_____

_____

If we allow them, our detours can bring hope and joy.

Now faith is confidence in what we hope for and assurance about what we do not see.

Hebrews 11:1

Friday

List five things for which you are grateful this week
and three things you learned from this week of study.

_____

_____

_____

_____

_____

_____

_____

_____

_____

_____

_____

_____

_____

_____

_____

_____

_____

_____

*Faith is the foundation that can motivate us to
seek joy in the midst of tragedy.*

Reflections from the Road

_____

_____

_____

_____

_____

_____

_____

_____

_____

_____

_____

_____

_____

_____

_____

_____

_____

_____

_____

_____

The enemy tempts us to remain in our grief and ignore the healing hand of the Lord.

Week 3

Notes

Notes

Paul and Timothy, servants of Christ Jesus,

Philippians 1:1

Monday

What feelings arise when you ponder the idea of being a doulos or slave to God?

_____

_____

_____

_____

_____

_____

_____

_____

_____

_____

_____

_____

_____

_____

_____

_____

Joy comes in humbly submitting to Christ as a "doulos."

Reflections from the Road

A spirit of humility leads us to seek the Lord before our feet hit the floor in the morning and before our head hits the pillow at night.

*Lord, I do not deserve to have you come
under my roof. But just say the word,
and my servant will be healed.
For I myself am a man under authority,
with soldiers under me.*

Matthew 8:8-9

Tuesday

Think of one thing you are worried about that is out of your control. Write a prayer, give it to God, and commit to leaving it with Him.

_____

_____

_____

_____

_____

_____

_____

_____

_____

_____

_____

_____

_____

_____

_____

_____

The responsibility for the world's well-being is not our burden.

Reflections from the Road

_____

_____

_____

_____

_____

_____

_____

_____

_____

_____

_____

_____

_____

_____

_____

_____

God is God, and we are not.

When someone invites you to a wedding feast,
do not take the place of honor.

For all those who exalt themselves will be
humbled,
and those who humble themselves will be
exalted."

Luke 14:8,11

Wednesday

Think of the day ahead: how can you uplift someone else while humbling yourself today?

_____
_____
_____
_____
_____
_____
_____
_____
_____
_____
_____
_____
_____
_____
_____
_____
_____
_____
_____

Great joy comes from knowing where to sit.

Reflections from the Road

_____

_____

_____

_____

_____

_____

_____

_____

_____

_____

_____

_____

_____

_____

_____

_____

_____

_____

_____

When you exalt yourself, you set yourself up to be humbled.

Every good and perfect gift is from above,
coming down from the Father
of the heavenly lights,
who does not change like shifting shadows.

James 1:16-17

Thursday

Write out today's verse below:

_____

_____

_____

_____

_____

_____

_____

_____

_____

_____

_____

_____

_____

_____

_____

_____

_____

_____

_____

_____

Stealing the victory ultimately steals the joy.

Reflections from the Road

Remembering the Giver of our success keeps it in the proper perspective.

Yet not as I will, but as you will.

Matthew 26:39

Friday

List five things for which you are grateful and
three things you learned from this week of study.

_____

_____

_____

_____

_____

_____

_____

_____

_____

_____

_____

_____

_____

_____

_____

_____

_____

Following the humble path of Jesus
is the ultimate road to joy.

Reflections from the Road

_____

_____

_____

_____

_____

_____

_____

_____

_____

_____

_____

_____

_____

_____

_____

Jesus Christ gave it all for you and me.
He humbled himself.

Week 4

Notes

Notes

"Anyone who loves me will obey my teaching."

John 14:23

Rejoice in the Lord and be glad,
you righteous;
sing, all you who are upright in heart!

Psalm 32:11

Monday

How do you know when you are headed down a path away from God's will? What are the warning signs?

_____

_____

_____

_____

_____

_____

_____

_____

_____

_____

_____

_____

_____

_____

_____

_____

_____

_____

Willful disobedience causes discontent and zaps our joy.

Reflections from the Road

Ignoring God's call can turn our peaceful calm seas into a tempestuous storm.

Therefore I tell you, do not worry about your life,
But seek first his kingdom and his righteousness,
and all these things will be given to you as well.
Therefore do not worry about tomorrow,
for tomorrow will worry about itself.
Each day has enough trouble of its own.

Matthew 6:25,33,34

Tuesday

Write out a prayer giving your specific worries to God and sign it. Treat this like a contract between you and God, honoring it and not taking back your worries.

_____

_____

_____

_____

_____

_____

_____

_____

_____

_____

_____

_____

_____

_____

_____

_____

We forfeit the joy of today by remembering the failures of yesterday and anticipating the unknown of tomorrow.

Reflections from the Road

_____

_____

_____

_____

_____

_____

_____

_____

_____

_____

_____

_____

_____

_____

_____

_____

_____

_____

_____

_____

_____

Jesus commands us to let go of worry.

*Blessed is the one whose transgressions
are forgiven,
whose sins are covered.*

*For day and night your hand was heavy on me;
my strength was sapped as in the heat of
summer.
Then I acknowledged my sin to you
and did not cover up my iniquity.
I said, "I will confess my transgressions to the
Lord."
And you forgave the guilt of my sin.*

Psalm 32:1-5

Wednesday

Is there someone from whom you need to ask forgiveness? Write a sincere apology, and make a plan to deliver the apology to them.

_____

_____

_____

_____

_____

_____

_____

_____

_____

_____

_____

_____

_____

_____

Joy comes not from a lack of sin but from our willingness to ask for forgiveness and our faith that the blood of Jesus cleanses us.

Reflections from the Road

_____

_____

_____

_____

_____

_____

_____

_____

_____

_____

_____

_____

_____

_____

_____

_____

_____

_____

_____

_____

_____

_____

_____

True joy comes when we admit our erroneous direction and correct our course.

Bear with each other
and forgive one another
if any of you has a grievance against someone.
Forgive as the Lord forgave you.
And over all these virtues put on love,
which binds them all together in perfect unity.

Colossians 3:13-14

Thursday

Write out today's verse below:

_____

_____

_____

_____

_____

_____

_____

_____

_____

_____

_____

_____

_____

_____

_____

_____

_____

_____

Let go of the grudge.

Reflections from the Road

God calls us to forgive and love each other in the same way that God forgives and loves us.

I care very little
if I am judged by you
or by any human court;
indeed, I do not even judge myself.
My conscience is clear,
but that does not make me innocent.
It is the Lord who judges me.

I Corinthians 4:3-4

Friday

List five things for which you are grateful
and three things you learned from this week of study.

_____

_____

_____

_____

_____

_____

_____

_____

_____

_____

_____

_____

_____

_____

_____

_____

_____

_____

True joy comes from pleasing God, not people.

Reflections from the Road

_____

_____

_____

_____

_____

_____

_____

_____

_____

_____

_____

_____

_____

_____

_____

_____

_____

_____

_____

_____

What if, instead of concentrating on pleasing people, I focused on pleasing God?

Week 5

Notes

Notes

*For even the Son of Man
did not come to be served,
but to serve,
and to give his life as a ransom for many.*

Mark 10:45

Monday

What feelings arise when you read about Florence and Timothy's service? Warmth? Guilt? Envy? Record your feelings here.

_____

_____

_____

_____

_____

_____

_____

_____

_____

_____

_____

_____

_____

_____

_____

_____

_____

_____

Jesus chose to be a servant.

Reflections from the Road

Lasting joy is more likely to come from serving than from being served.

[M]ake my joy complete by being like-minded,
having the same love,
being one in spirit and of one mind.
Do nothing out of selfish ambition or vain
conceit.
Rather, in humility value others above
yourselves,
not looking to your own interests
but each of you to the interests of the others.

Philippians 2:2-4

Tuesday

In what areas of your life do you feel most selfless?
In what areas are you most selfish?
How can you be more selfless in your problem areas?

_____

_____

_____

_____

_____

_____

_____

_____

_____

_____

_____

_____

_____

_____

_____

_____

_____

*We are most content when we follow
Jesus's example of selfless love.*

Reflections from the Road

Selflessly helping others brings happiness.

I can do all this through him who gives me strength.

Philippians 4:13

Where do you need God's strength this week? Write
out a prayer asking Him to provide it to you.

_____
_____
_____
_____
_____
_____
_____
_____
_____
_____
_____
_____
_____
_____
_____

Immeasurable strength comes from God and will be renewed when it is invested back into His service.

Reflections from the Road

_____

_____

_____

_____

_____

_____

_____

_____

_____

_____

_____

_____

_____

_____

_____

_____

When we use the strength and power from God
for the glory of God,
we are investing it wisely.

*Therefore encourage one another
and build each other up,
just as in fact you are doing.*

I Thessalonians 5:11

Thursday

Write out today's verse below.

_____

_____

_____

_____

_____

_____

_____

_____

_____

_____

_____

_____

_____

_____

_____

_____

_____

_____

The beauty of being an encourager is that everyone can do it.

Reflections from the Road

_____

_____

_____

_____

_____

_____

_____

_____

_____

_____

_____

_____

_____

_____

_____

_____

_____

_____

_____

_____

_Encouragers have the ability
to fundamentally change lives._

I planted the seed,
Apollos watered it,
but God has been making it grow.
So neither the one who plants
nor the one who waters is anything,
but only God, who makes things grow.
The one who plants and
the one who waters have one purpose,
and they will each be rewarded
according to their own labor.

I Corinthians 3:5-9

Friday

List five things for which you are grateful this week and three things you learned from this week of study.

_____
_____
_____
_____
_____
_____
_____
_____
_____
_____
_____
_____
_____
_____
_____
_____

Our joy cannot be dependent on the actions of others.

Reflections from the Road

_____

_____

_____

_____

_____

_____

_____

_____

_____

_____

_____

_____

_____

_____

_____

_____

_____

_____

_____

_____

_____

When we are mentoring others for Christ,
we are not judged on the results.

Week 6

Notes

Notes

We love because he first loved us.

I John 4:19

*And hope does not put us to shame,
because God's love has been poured out into
our hearts through the Holy Spirit, who has
been given to us.*

Romans 5:5

Monday

What feelings arise when you read today's verses about how much
God loves you? Do you feel worthy or unworthy?
Write out your feelings here.

_____

_____

_____

_____

_____

_____

_____

_____

_____

_____

_____

_____

_____

_____

_____

_____

_____

*God loves us so much that He wants to move in
with us.*

Reflections from the Road

There is nothing we can do to make God love us any more or any less.

But very truly I tell you,
it is for your good that I am going away.
Unless I go away, the Advocate will not come
to you;
but if I go, I will send him to you.

John 16:7

Now is your time of grief, but I will see you
again and you will rejoice, and no one will
take away your joy.
Ask and you will receive, and your joy will be
complete.

John 16:22,24

Tuesday

What questions do you have about the Holy Spirit? Do you find the concept confusing or hopeful?

_____

_____

_____

_____

_____

_____

_____

_____

_____

_____

_____

_____

_____

_____

_____

_____

We must take the initiative to use this transformational power of the Holy Spirit within us.

Reflections from the Road

_____

_____

_____

_____

_____

_____

_____

_____

_____

_____

_____

_____

_____

_____

_____

_____

When we accept Jesus Christ as our Lord
and Savior, the Holy Spirit comes and dwells
in us.

Rejoice always,
pray continually,
give thanks in all circumstances;
for this is God's will for you in Christ Jesus.
Do not quench the Spirit.

I Thessalonians 5:16-19

Wednesday

Have you ever had to walk away from an old
version of yourself? How did that feel?

_____

_____

_____

_____

_____

_____

_____

_____

_____

_____

_____

_____

_____

_____

_____

_____

_____

_____

*The Holy Spirit amplifies God's power
available within us to refresh and revitalize.*

Reflections from the Road

_____

_____

_____

_____

_____

_____

_____

_____

_____

_____

_____

_____

_____

_____

_____

_____

_____

_____

_____

_____

_____

_____

The Spirit infuses us with the power to live a vibrant Christ-centered life.

Further, my brothers and sisters,
rejoice in the Lord!
It is no trouble for me to write
the same things to you again,
and it is a safeguard for you.

Philippians 3:1

Thursday

Write out today's verse below:

_____

_____

_____

_____

_____

_____

_____

_____

_____

_____

_____

_____

_____

_____

With the Holy Spirit impacting our hearts from within us, we can have the glow of God radiating out from inside us, giving us freedom and life.

Reflections from the Road

_____

_____

_____

_____

_____

_____

_____

_____

_____

_____

_____

_____

_____

_____

_____

_____

_____

_____

_____

_____

_____

The Holy Spirit allows us to see God more clearly and to develop into a person resembling Christ.

But the fruit of the Spirit is love, joy, peace, forbearance, kindness, goodness, faithfulness, gentleness and self-control.

Galatians 5:22-23

Friday

List five things for which you are grateful this week
and three things you learned from this week of study.

_____

_____

_____

_____

_____

_____

_____

_____

_____

_____

_____

_____

_____

_____

_____

_____

_____

_____

*Through the power of the Spirit, we produce a
concatenation of Christian graces, including joy.*

Reflections from the Road

_____

_____

_____

_____

_____

_____

_____

_____

_____

_____

_____

_____

_____

_____

_____

_____

_____

_____

_____

_____

When we walk in step with the Holy Spirit,
we can expect the Spirit to naturally produce
the "fruit of the Spirit."

Week 7

Notes

Notes

But our citizenship is in heaven.
And we eagerly await a Savior from there,
the Lord Jesus Christ,

Philippians 3:20

Monday

Listen to "I'll Fly Away" and "The World Is Not My Home." How do these songs make you feel?

_____

_____

_____

_____

_____

_____

_____

_____

_____

_____

_____

_____

_____

_____

_____

_____

_____

_____

Look forward to the joy and promise of heaven.

Reflections from the Road

The cares and tribulations of this world are temporary and do not compare to the joy and riches we will have in heaven.

Do not let your hearts be troubled.
You believe in God; believe also in me.
My Father's house has many rooms;
if that were not so, would I have told you
that I am going there to prepare a place for
you?

John 14:1-2

Tuesday

Put yourself into the mindset of a conquering citizen, such as a Babylonian. Now picture yourself as a conquered citizen, like one of the Israelites. How different do the two perspectives feel?

_____

_____

_____

_____

_____

_____

_____

_____

_____

_____

_____

_____

_____

_____

_____

_____

_____

The joy awaiting us is unimaginable.

Reflections from the Road

The believer's eternal citizenship is set in a secure place with privileges too great for us to even imagine.

*Whatever happens,
conduct yourselves in a
manner worthy of the gospel of Christ.*

Philippians 1:27

Wednesday

Do you ever feel like you're "living for this world?"
How can you shift your mindset?

_____

_____

_____

_____

_____

_____

_____

_____

_____

_____

_____

_____

_____

_____

_____

Let us live our lives worthy of our impending citizenship.

Reflections from the Road

Believers should live as citizens of a kingdom in which they are not physically located.

*For to me, to live is Christ
and to die is gain.*

*I am torn between the two:
I desire to depart and be with Christ,
which is better by far;
but it is more necessary
for you that I remain in the body.*

Philippians 1:21,23,24

Thursday

Write out today's verse below:

_____
_____
_____
_____
_____
_____
_____
_____
_____
_____
_____
_____
_____
_____
_____
_____
_____
_____

Rejoice in the opportunities to glorify God as we actively wait on the Lord.

Reflections from the Road

_____

_____

_____

_____

_____

_____

_____

_____

_____

_____

_____

_____

_____

_____

_____

_____

_____

_____

After our salvation, God leaves us here on the earth to do His work.

Today, if you hear his voice,
do not harden your hearts.

Hebrews 4:7

Friday

List five things for which you are grateful this week and three things you learned from this week of study.

_____

_____

_____

_____

_____

_____

_____

_____

_____

_____

_____

_____

_____

_____

_____

Today is the day to journey to joy.

Reflections from the Road

_____

_____

_____

_____

_____

_____

_____

_____

_____

_____

_____

_____

_____

_____

_____

_____

_____

_____

_____

When you feel the nudge of the Lord, don't wait.

Although the journey should last a lifetime, our seven-week voyage has ended.

What are three things that made an impact on your journey?

Did you have any preconceived notions about joy that were not biblically based? What were they, and how has your vision changed?

What is the most important thing you carried away from this journey?

Look back on your goals from Week One, which have you accomplished and which will you be continuing to work on?

Thank you for journeying and journaling with us!

We have traveled through seven weeks with the Word of God and the God of the Word. We pray that God blesses your journey, bringing you closer to your Lord and Savior.

Please let us know which of the weeks resonated with you? Which were most challenging? Please tell us about your journey. You can reach us at www.younggalla.com or www.leighwyoung.com.

If you are interested in hosting a *Journey to Joy* Bible Study for your church or women's group or if you would like to participate in one, please email Leigh@youngandassociates.com. You can also call 828.691.0586. YouTubes for the study are located at https://www.youtube.com/c/LeighYoung.

May God bless you as you rejoice in Him!

Joyfully yours,
Kathryn and Leigh

Made in the USA
Coppell, TX
09 February 2023

12422202R00072